Thought[...]n
An Hourglass

Dustin Alexander

For Jacky, my wife, my always
For Poe, who showed me life is
full of poetry and stories

Contents

III. Ingenuity

IV. Transition

I. Thoughts Seen In An Hourglass

The Castle I Live In Is Made Of Sand

Cutting me, the skin reacts as if it was sponge
The mind opened like peeled skin of an orange
Pray my heart is not made of stone
Or frozen from the years gone by
Do not let it wash away
It is a fragile thing we built
Upon the fragile ground we hope for it to remain

This me that is so many things
Granite are the legs to see whatever would be the end
Brittle are the moments that are together with strength
Don't let it wash away
This castle made of sand

As I've only found it to live
Never before have I questioned my existence
Now I've found my place
Built on a beach far away
It stands opposite from a lighthouse
Meant to beckon only its solitude

Only so it remains
These strange parts have begun to work
No longer the challenge, they are better than believed normalcy
The windows not views like prison cells
Instead an expanse of sand as beautiful as flowers

The clapping sound of water only heard, applauding the stars that
never left

Do not let it be known
This place of mine
The water to dare forward
To take a world away with the tide
For the castle I live in is made of sand

Maiden

Maiden what name did they give you
 What was the real one, hasn't mattered in years
Then what was taken when they gave it to you
What could she say?
To these questions, if your voice doesn't matter to them
Given birth to bred, never taught how to live
No to standing on your feet, equal footing in anything, it still hasn't
been
Maiden they think you're a product of the world
Forgetting how you have given the world to them
Instead of darkness as thoughts
Drifted from oblivion to the specs of eternity in between
Where has it taken you since?
Can anything be given?
After the denial of everything
Where will you walk maiden, how will you
Free or as an effect, searching for a tormentor
Speak and tell what has happened
Let it be the closing chapter
Instead of an odyssey, a suffering saga with no end

We The Perplexed

The needle injects into the apple that we're eating
The face is droopy now hanging, miles on us we haven't tread
But we're busy shouting now, choosing a name we proclaim will
smite the other that disagrees with us
We've become we believe so many things, far too many things to notice

Coughing in our house, regulations are shrugs checked off, the
sweet home killing us
But our precious moments are spent finding new ways to ignore
each other
Connect without connecting
A roll of sadness read off by the smiling bleached figure on the screen
To eyes and ears that have seen it all

Their dying aches are proof of this
No doctor is willing to touch them, going further is not on the agenda
All of us are on the chopping board
Those lonely nights screaming for help, no loss of sleep to those that
wouldn't know how to begin to care

The freezing man opens his broken window to allow the air
He closes his eyes to a world that has been hard on him
But not nearly as hard as he is on himself
The children are killing each other, there's no report from a distant
land, when it's all a step out of the open door
All in listening distance

Perplexing as it is we've never seized to give time to clear it up
A greater confusion than, a greater tale than of how we circle
ourselves down the drain

You can speak what you want but they're allowed to listen
Take heart if you are sad when you believe no one else is
Underestimate and oversee
Thoughtless and disease find their way through
There's no one to look for this particular cure
Power assumed beyond our grasps, waiting for those hidden in their
fortresses, waiting for them to control
The hands they are many, are not many anymore

The only thing to change this, to give a slither of hope is what
breaks the silence between the two loved ones
If it ever comes
How did we get this way or what have we always been
We claim we don't know
We claim we can't understand, not when we are the perplexed

Hard To Believe

They'd come with their knees on eggshells
The sort they'd force others to stand and walk on for so many years
Weakness there plea for forgiveness
Crying wolf that no one believes
Even if the beast was breathing by the open door

All the things they kept, offering only empty plates
Years have proved they hadn't know what was in front of them
The worse of their suspicions were true
Ironic that they had been the cause of it

Aid they need from those left on the curb
Silence in response if there hope in assistance is true
 The only excuses that they now make is for why they did the
opposite of what they were told to
It's hardy for sympathy to come when they show what lives in their
core every day
With lies still reigning as king and to all those that they were sup-
posed to love, treated as nothing but peasants

What Is The Danger?

What is the danger?
The man or the gun
Can satisfaction be guaranteed?
Without it's firing

Strengths from it
Threats from it
The person though could be overcome
Though it's them that makes the decision
Marching through the neighborhood
Labeling them dangerous

By finding a target
All places innocent
Until corrupted by human indifference
What is the danger?

Five thunderclaps from fired shots
Are from the final heartbeats of the victim
Bleeding down the cracks and crevices of the eroded street
Some suppressed voice
Just trying to wish it all away
What is the danger?

Sounds tune our ears to forced familiar
Sirens speak of what's passed as they race toward the incident
Eyes hide behind windows allowing the gunmen to see the street as
a lonely thing
A thing in which to taint

Yet if they were not the force behind the firing weapon?
If it was certainty and amusement in their eyes, of victory
Plummeting our minutes into chaos, no matter where we hide,
matter of time
The hand never empty but what if they could fail without it
What if there was silence from this for one evening
What is the danger?

The Problems No One Wants to Care About

The drying rivers and the drying oceans is a song
Of how much we don't care, if it isn't a press of a button about us
then it isn't of interest
The cracks in our heart or where there is sand where there should
be blood pumping
It's as gone as the sympathy for anyone passing, known, unknown,
famous or otherwise
A thing with a strangle hold on us, just waiting for us to struggle
when we realize it has its hands around our throat

We spin, do we spin? We connect and are divided and war despite
the changes either side could bring
We look to the sky but feel less worrisome of the meteor of truth
approaching
We don't communicate verbally face to face anymore, if we ever
have and yet
There are problems and yet they are the same
Problems no one wants to talk about, problems no one wants to
care about

Like the thought that could drive you mad
So you push it away but perhaps it had been sanity telling you that
you've live a life of insanity
That you can always find the root of it, maybe if you don't discuss it
with the others so eager to push it all away
Maybe you can just follow it then the feeling wouldn't be as miser-
able as it now
Maybe it wouldn't revisit like the nightmare that does not need
sleep, like the nightmare that does not need to ever wake

The taste of rights upon our lips and tongue and the right to deny
others the same
All from the same voice that stopped screaming loud for one thing
and begun to whisper on another
One and one are never two because we find all the reasons to say so
Annals of time played their tune, you can mock, you can ignore but
when all are long gone it continues its notes
It sings its song
Shocks and surprises the way people live their life although it's been
the same even in the doorways of open and closed doors
But we have the power to say it cannot be so, we can purge against
them, rally anytime they can take a breath, these things we rather
not say
Just the way we can hold a sign at funeral because we feel we
knew the way a person lived their life

It's not an outrage, it's not even news
It's just a thing accepted and to be able to swallow at its most sickening
The voices won't like that any speak it, the statues in minds crumble
It doesn't stop it from being true, it doesn't stop them from purging
and condemning all that know it
The problems no one cares about
They are small ones, they are large ones
They are all enormous and grow the longer they are avoided

A smile that isn't real, a hatred that only is
As enormous as the person that kills for any same reason they felt
worth it
There are no rights and wrongs in necessity they say however all
has become necessity
That's the world we have to swallow?
Just like the ones scrubbing the floors for minimum wage, the ones
that work harder than the ones who walk it

The ones that wanted to paint, to study to save a life, to dream an infinite dream
But instead they worry if the healthcare will ever let them be seen
Not just for them but for their children
If they'll have a good education
So they can afford to dream when there never should have been a cost to begin with
When so many told them they couldn't
If all these things to think and question are crazy then let me be the mad man
For that is what I'll be right now

I am the mad man
For my thoughts
For the concerns around us
The shed of blood, the death of land, the life span of our single planet, the girl who wants to hope with a butterfly in her hand
The remainder of us, our emotion and what becomes of it
I am the mad man
For I stress the problems no one wants to talk about
The answers that cannot be given by a smile through sharp teeth, a stab in the back, a cruel play for status, it is all so insignificant to the reaper who if only he had nickel
 For all who claimed they had it

I am the mad man
For hoping that hope exists for once
That things are brought to our attention just in time
Not always when it's too late, when things are at their worst, when it is all doom
Only then when it is news
I am the mad man for being sane
In a world I wish as such

Not for any group of thought except the one where we exist, we must!
Where we can step away from it long enough to see the problems
The problems we are afraid of, for that is what it is among the millions of things, it is fear
Things that needed talking, the thing that needs facing
The problems that no one wants to talk about

What A Fine Morning

I know it may not seem like it
The start of the dripping of all its details
Imagine gutter and sewers
Drowning sounds as they drain

But even so we've always known better
The value of a moment that we've seen squandered and regretted
It's to this moment that I share with you

The silent rush
Sounds of scratches revealing themselves with a coin
Not for the big payout perhaps just a small pot of gold
Something simply to continue

The dominance of bleach
So early there's no one to know it's clean
No one to say thank you or be grateful
So many moments saying we're long past that
The urge to have done more, should have done more, ever waiting

It's to this morning I offer you in slumber and when awake
A morning that doesn't have to know it's just beginning
A fine morning that asks nothing in return

The Tireless Worker

From dawn to the first ring of the morning
Hardly a chance to sit on the edge of the bed
A simple choice of inaction would be met with a mountain of
consequences
She toils with hands strong, maintain their shape though the lines cut
into their palm
Early she goes into work and late she leaves
Though energy seems depleted at her return
It could hardly be seen from an expression that is a foe of exhaustion
A smile on her face searching the smile of others
Of the lives in her hands, the simple joy of their happiness
Sweeter than the finest cake, more rewarding than the determined
green paper
A different ruler she measures by
Lending a hand when the hour can give no more in minutes
She finds it still lost in some previous time scape we lived in
Offering hers, one that is strong
Gratitude is absent, though she'd hardly know what it looks like
Having looked away if the moment presented itself
Tireless she may be but far more than a worker
 Far cry from a drone
More than it was taught to her even long after the world changed
for the better
Never for this reason was it done
Fires that were great have burned out for reasons such as that
Love questioned and lost
It's a simple reason, more than a foundation of home could offer
Aiding a hand to those too scared to asked for one
Could be written off as a stranger, an unknown

For this tireless as she is the protecting figure
The mother of generations of those that come to meet her
Reasons like this she is like no other
To eyes that have seen it so long it may go unnoticed
Living in this world she turns for their benefit
But to truly be blind would be impossible, the eyes eventually see
Her greatest efforts are to be chronicled in something heavier than stone
For her it has always been so
Appreciation can never be paid with anything but love

Grey Turning Black

Of all the mountains of darkness behind us
Not a light of life in this slope, this descent
Home in the distance turned off their glimmer
For home could be the season of rain, cloud like hands moving the
blinds for possible sunshine
Or the crack of sky to earth turning black
Safe with lamplight and man made
Distant from the mountains of black
Of rolling in unseen, only to roll in some more
To the illumination of an ancient sun past its age, the entire city
before it
Above it a cloud of toxic uncertainty
A delusion that had been its creator
The unaware moving around in it
Suffocation a daily activity, easier to appear a mystery, except it
cannot be with this view
Such make those the stumped, with hand under chin like chiseled by
Rodin
On the curb of the streets no one really knows the names or the
footsteps their walking over
So where does this lead this grey of day, this extinguished night?
The complete black behind us
Where life rest under its care
Where is the real sunshine to go with the night?
Where is the whole, that shouldn't seem as frightening?
Closed eyes sealed up is a fate resisted but can make amends
Going forward though, seeing it as more is the greatest obstacle
The battler of fate and predestined acceptance
Where does the grey turn black?
And form there come the other true half

The Color of Our Skin

Where are you wisdom for I am looking for you?
Behind the lines of inequality
The near exact shades that have been excuses
For teaching each other apart

What wonders line within the truth?
Of the myth of understanding

Could it free us from the history of everything?
That had etched our division so deeply
That we are ashamed of and complain
That we still riot when shown today

What are the answers to what puzzle our legacies?
Red strings connecting us all
Hail future solutions
Just if we looked beyond the shades

Only worn to where the body had been born, only adapting our
many possibilities
Showing us our adaptability, followed from the beginning, showing
us it's surviving beauty
A connection to us wanting to continue as human beings.

The finger pointing has lost its direction
And progress has lost its sense of torch carriers
That stop to promote the problems of the beginning
Only to scare them into being unending

To understand something so simple
Only in final minutes of a devastating ending
Would be characteristic of our wish to continue
To see a face in everything, to wish it all in our image

As desire that should come with pride
If we can learn to live with that image
If we can understand that these small changes are our completion
Our great leap forward yearned in even the greatest of doubters
Would become a reality worth living in

Through The Thorn Fields

Caught as we ran rippled cloth like banners beside us
Drawn blood left a trail
From whence we came
Through every grit we run forward
Least we face the place we flee

All in black is the winged building
Please allow the sun to come in, speckled if it must
Through the wild fields of torn and snare

If I'd find my way out I'd bring you to a world of fresh born
flowers
Nothing wilted growing thorns
That is what I whisper to myself amidst the voices
To wish away anything else
Reaching to take my hand, its cutting grip

Avoid the blood soaked tips
It's through the field I'm sure a world away from here
One where panic is unspoken

The moving gates a prison no longer
Better to find a field worth being buried
No matter how low the bones, it could feel the warmth
Or greater yet a field to stand on proud of living, a field to wait for you
A field never again to be alone

Sap

The body has woken to every bone aching
Every joint yelling, every sound a knuckle crack
The strength is behind a fogged window
No way to know it, no way to reach it
Sapped of the life and energy displayed around you
Time is not the culprit
The brittle state is something greater
As its stealing moments in a life meant to be the peak
I come to you skin hanging off the bones
Temper riled like a lion, the state of me a ruffled mane
A dejected doubtful soul whose saw no directions, no roads taking
Still I knew my road to you
You see me and question an end to come soon
Or is it a spirit sapped of something essential and taken but not lost
forever
In this belief flesh feels to evolve from the progression of rotting in
a living vessel
To the strength of a thousand oceans
Sinking mountains with palms, braving winds of hurricanes with
playful expressions on my face
It's you that takes me to the thoughts to fill a thousand minds,
unbound in a time, an era
Stretching out to no end
More than what is returned, something else given
It has been what has been missing
A warmth of a thousand hearts in one to go with it
The fire of my own you've given though I've handed it to you
It is yours an igniting, something only just beginning

The Useless Things That Mean Everything to Us

They line our shelves, they corner our memories and they mean
nothing to anyone but you and me
For them it will be boxed and shipped
Excavated and close us out
As if we are the last paragraph of a chapter, the eager reader
hardly finishing and turning our page towards another
To us it's something we couldn't imagine
Taking a room of existence and giving it to strangers
Closing the door without caring
Wearing the black to mourn without knowing
Things that hung from us that we kept
A meaning between us to make us smile through everyday trouble
Task at hand, killing precious time when our minds were only of
each other, of returning to the long awaited home together
A thing to steady us but not always able to dominate the feeling of
anxiety, of being far away
Only because its power was strongest when we were with each other
Everything that lines the shelf, worn or hung that tell a story
Everything they believe useless and ready to shut a door to
Everything that had meaning to us

Do You Want to Disappear?

A challenge from the daily
The hush words you never say
For the act is easy
If you wish it the world is a master of the trick
Forgotten a shame but sometimes a freedom
Desired remote then a closer reality
The supposed everyday becomes a farce
Just as when the earth turns itself over

That of which you cling to has more worth than it may appear at
the moment
You will not find it with them, they've never been sure the meaning
Could never truly tell you if you exist
Do you want to disappear?
Simply wish it first and then follow the feeling
The voice on the track that stops suddenly
It'll be a thin air vanishing act

Mountains and Valleys

You'll do great things
So they said when you were younger
When the scent was fresh, scattered and drenched
Before the clouds shifted upon what appeared shiftless

As the truth pulled closer to whisper a secret
Everything changes
So it spoke during the sight of those years in youth
Watching others crumble before you
Holding steadfast believing the words told
Like scarfs wrapped around you to keep you safe from the cold
raw Earth

How were the words, dry on the tongue, blood on the cracked lips?
Like a lullaby drifting you to sleep or keeping you suppressed in a
dream you never wish to wake
Oh the mountains you'll move
The valleys filled from all those that never could

Now it's your concern too
You wonder of the truth of this
Is your life significant because you live it?
For the reason that the world is viewed from your eyes
That perhaps their words that are in your thoughts had turned to
promises
Were just that, just words, as easy to grasp as air
As different as a raindrops during a downpour

Perhaps this playful melody, the one you didn't know you wanted to hear
Like sirens luring you to belief
That you should stand on a plateau
How your feet are sunk in as theirs
That youthful vigor, skin and time have turned to face you
They are the opposing stranger
Decades it's been, doubts abound and second choices are made
So that they live around you
How do these words sound now?
A squeak in a tunnel, a thud in a forest

Have they still their invincibility?
Or is it as if you were laying down not sitting up when told
Clenching your legs with eager, instead in a state of immobilization
Creating the sound of twirling your thumbs
Enduring the winters only to prepare for them again

Night and day blink in front of you
It had seemed you were led astray
Like a maze masked as a straight path
But the guide it seems was of your creation

Now you see things with open eyes
Afraid those words had long since disappeared into the depths of imagination
You repeat them now in the closed walls of the shed
Where the masses walk unaware
In the sound of screams day to day

To the lives that race by in a place strange to you
To this view that covers the view of valleys left to you
 And the mountains still unmoved

The Boy That Wished For More

In his earliest days
The boy ran, at the time, to any beckon, any call
To those unworthy
Yet he tried not to know entirely
He hung by their side so he was not lonely
But lonely was all he felt, mocked, blamed, singled out and framed
As a picture of something he never desired to be
Locked in a cage in his mind
Locked in a cage in his soul

Long days and short days down this mistaken road
A pass up from one shadow to the other, worsens the further
Until it nearly broke the boy
The boy that wished for more
Until he realized without realizing it
That surrounding himself with those beyond all he saw
Made him again feel human
That he mattered, that he was more
And the boy that ran when beckoned was gone
The always empty, lost in soul and direction boy was gone
For now he knew, what he'd wished for

What Would My Authors Say

Its night, they're forced to leave among the cigarettes and the mutual feelings, on the pretty staircase that no one pays attention too, the blocked flight where the roof would lead them to the stars, would let them see an expanse of possibilities. Huddled they open the book, trying to have the pages save them, guide them, wondering what the authors would say if only they could speak to them.

Among the metal they're shivering, where everything moves, it was a long trek to sleep another night upon this place. Some nights they wonder if the blanket over their head will make the night vanish faster and bring day in its place, some nights all they can do is turn a page, hoping it will keep them company, sometimes here at their lowest they wonder what the authors would say

They're welcomed upon a place that wants them cast out, outsiders don't belong in a realm of schemers and lairs. They make sure that every day before is as uncomfortable as possible and for good measure, cut out what little they could call their own. It leaves them alone and in those moments of uncertainty of where will they go, they turn the page and wonder what would the authors say

In a hospital room with someone in its bed, in between moments they look toward the book for company, only able to concentrate once every few minutes which is really hours. Even in these moments they are not allowed the comfort to breathe. I wonder what would the authors say?

If they manifested, if the authors appeared before them, would they move the hand from their face. Would they smile and laugh at the complaints and tell them worse, would they sit down and listen even give them some advice. Would their words be like their pages, hopefully even more, it's to wonder in these moments, moments that make up a lifetime, what would the authors say?

Star Traverser

They had come to sit in front of us
Near the oak desk with a cup beside them with no thirst
Though they would drink it none the less
To keep their hands busy as they speak

It was the comfort that one hour had against the other
They remembered laying in their bed beside their beloved
 An then another hour out beyond their home
A space where all the stars were clearer

Not out of reach because you weren't reaching
That was when the first feeling came they said
They wore an unending exposure of suffering to truth
No matter what emotion they had or what happen their reach from
the things that glimmered in space, planets and stars and moons and
suns was something beyond far, beyond out of reach, it was nonexistent
There would be no anger or laughter for their pain
Sadness and joy there would be nothing

As they moved by their own hand, in their own accord
Never before had they felt as alone as to know there could be no
world for them let alone one that could care
Not out there in the illuminated dark, not as a traverser of the stars
Where one's fate held no weight to its observer
They huddled their cup as if speaking of a nightmare that was had
Looking in the eyes of the person as they spoke, nothing hidden, no
last attempt in concealments except for the small amount of smoke
from the cup they cradled

How could the eyes see it even through the smoke, even if it was clear, how could they understand it
Surviving and achieving meant little compared to this realization
For what did anything measure compared to a quiet place without empathy

All The Worlds Are Gathering Dust

Pulling the point of grey in the night
Passing the severed ties, knotted strings that go on forever
Observing the things that are endless, long beyond me crumbling on
this day
Deep galaxies away and completely in arms reach
As all the worlds are gathering dust
In them my place is a question
One I search for, a powerful voice, inside my self
One to justify my existence, one to finally give me content in
As the things that once seemed forever beyond me, all of them had
been waiting for tonight
Before they are covered away, in darkness, in the assumption of
nothing
I am freed in order to ask why
All the worlds are gathering dust and yet somehow I am still here

To The Distant Shore

The lights are moving, searching the waves in between
We are on the sands, we have yet to begin
It can be seen as a dark behemoth
It can been seen as anything to keep us here, our feet planted and
always wondering
But it will never cure the yearning we know, the one that moves
through us like blood, as if it demands our heart to beat solely for it
Never answering the questions that will haunt us for all our lives
It is not a dream if we believe only with half our heart
For it means we only believe in half our life

II. Night Lullabies

Mirror Walker

Have you ever seen reflections through the mirror?
When the mirror looks into the mirror behind you
Cast down in a realm of infinite reflection
Wondering what worlds it would take you if you traveled them
Does it shake your nerves to wonder?
If in the furthest infinite
There was something there perhaps, staring back wondering the same
If it could move forward the way you wondered if you could move back
Would it be content to simply pass through?
Or would it show itself to be something horrible
Shattering every reflection as it approached you

Story of The Winged Girl

The winged girl, she'd stared at the world for some time
Seen the changes, gave advice to those that watched as well
Until her voice was silent with sound, having fallen on deaf ears
So she wore the modern world, hid her wings but never tore them off
Trying to figure what she hadn't for centuries
Her place in the world
Others she would see, those that had wandered away too
How would they recognize her now?
The wings hidden in her jacket
The face like another in the crowd
For everyone is searching as she is,
For a way for their voice to resonate again and be heard

Gargoyles

Light dawns
The light teased on the stone
As it would on the skin
Sentinels guard on edges
As time burns and wanes

Observers of the plain
Naked truth of the world
A wash away many times
Sometimes a drench
Soft like fade to things left to remain

There can be no hiding
From the eyes of the still
The unmoving but the watching
In the place with the clearest view

A Silent Man

She'd lived with the man for some time
The late night whispers were assumed prayers
Self-urging for early slumber
Perhaps even dreamless sleep

But restlessness caused tossing and turning
Eyes open to the voices, the tongue something unheard
Slur, in the soft voice, indistinguishable in its tongue's play of shadows
Then the aches came to her

The sound of joints crackling that she had used to hear from the
foot dragging, pacing
Was now heard from her, the steps she still heard, as if they were
moving further away
Now seemed to be coming for her
Escape impossibility had been why the voice spoke to itself
The cause of all these late nights

These were prayers to take her away from herself
She was trapped in the thin walled room
Hearing blocked away, escape for the holes the words still came through
The voice she heard seemed to scream for mercy, it was raspy,
dashed and severed

The ankles and legs and back were her pain now not his
The world was dimming for her the way it had once for him
Age and days stolen away
Taken by the silent man who managed to steal time away

All that is left is memory, she'd had it once, seeing it now though
fade away
Without a way to question now, it had become difficult
It would be hard now for the eyes to even tell the difference
Grey where color had been
To see what she had lost

The Feast

Pour the heart into a bowl
Let them all gather around and taste
Let them say as parts of it are stuck between their teeth, that there
is no soul
No random comparisons, no clever way to hide itself in words

To be honest and straightforward, too dark
It could be a song if it wasn't what it was
Watch as it pumps and beats, wishing it could regain its rhythms
taken away
Watch despite all that's been said

Tell me if it is not a heart
That pours it's feelings out
Tell me the reason for it not to feel
In this feast of merciless tasting

Folk Song

In an unknown land
As mysterious as any
To where the fire is the center, to keep us warm
Stories have given way to expression
Sound of every chord flavored in a different nation

The longing of home for all of us yet the yearning to be here
Plays a song more complete, one never heard
To the percussion of the flame, tips leave in orange orbs
Lost in any direction, drifting ever slow
The song plays encouragement, claps of hard hands

Explain all our sleepless nights
To be without a final hour
We're taken away, traversed in the place
Born in rooms with windows
Always wondering if there was something greater

Greener than the grass could have imagined
Closer than a lover's kiss
It's the folk song we swore we never heard
It's the first we ever learned
Sounds that leave profound patterns in their wake
Not strangers gathered round, no shame as the music takes over
the conversation
We've been here before, it's always been our place of creation

The Folded Man

For every layer folding in itself
What I am is not consolidated
Surely it is clearer what you see
What makes me cry, what makes me smile?
My desires in all their glory whether in a field of sunflowers, rays of light
Or in the dead wasteland of cold metal and rust
Surely you see it as I become smaller
Slowly it folds from all sides of me
I am floating, I am the center, a final square
No longer bound by the concept of gravity
Can you hear my voice?
What it says, anything that could coat it, hide it, is gone
Just the bare me that was in every shed of tear, every gleam of hope

Bone Shifting

Through the rain beaten window
As clear as if it was in front of me
Her face, her comfort
The ease on my mind, wind of serenity
The unclenching from under the bone, from under the jaw

To electric storm of the mind
Her hand under it, moving under my chin
Kindness that knows no exhaustion
Who I am always shifting
Wanting to become all the more reason she's smiling

The Shadow Clock

A quarter of time cut away
Examined under the microscope of experience
Is anything measured as it really is?
A slice is larger than the other, the distance of the sun seems
equally further
The moments are hesitant
Enlarged beneath me, lost in its cast
To measure it I can hear a different ticking
At night the water dropping
Buckets of hours, drops of minutes
A guess would need more than a mirror
A shadow is deceptive, how do I declare this precise moment
This deciding factor against the wish of others to slip away
Lost in a greater cast net, when night comes, when its reach is
everywhere
How could we know it was lost?
Is it these brimming questions, these still moments, a trace back
upon reflection?

In The Shadow Of Christmas

Beyond the neon lights
Far from the advertisements
Sales and rushes, maddening looks in the eyes of customers
Far from caroling, where it could still be heard these days

The image of fireplace and family
Snowed in airports and dinners
In the shadow of Christmas
So many still remain

Feeble hands, the lonely, for who it is just another moment to pass
The sick and the passing whose lives will be overshadowed
By the waiting children and presents
By the time to be merry that have in many respects seized to be merry
In the shadows of Christmas

They wait too far to feel the imagined warmth of the red and green lights
Too far to feel what they might be sole heirs to feel
The true meaning of Christmas long forgot

Temple

I dare not climb it
Up above to what the pillars hold
To a platform to look above
Where hanging is the ivory moon

Dozens of doorways and rooms
I wonder are there any tombs
Are there people I know, those I've buried?

Thinking of things of which makes the temple stand
My sacred, my only
To here, thoughts are kept that are special
Dreams even more so, vivid and possible

There's a fear of stepping out
Something beyond the knowledge that is found in here
Voices whisper of similar thoughts
Similar dreams, it makes the temple seem hollow

Its endless halls, its isolated understanding
Becomes a mixed incomprehension
Begging for the feeling of its existence
Yet surely it would not be a life outside for me

Only inside the temple
One way to look outside
That is with thoughts, of assumptions, engineered by imagination
All I've found though is it is not enough

Something I desire to see waits for me
For a moment I leave the corridors

My friends, my lover
The endless walk that does not poke holes in knowledge I've found
I leave this, I say to myself only a moment
To climb the long set of stairs

An easier path in mazes of many
To the outside air of the rooftops
The air greets with a breeze, more than I imagined
But I choose not to look down upon the rest of the world from
where I stand

It's only to realize again the purpose of my humble wandering within
Towards the temple I've built of my thoughts, of everything
Something to look upon, to confirm
The only witness I need
The ivory moon that hangs above me

Hauntings

The doors are locked, they're witness to your waiting for death
The sap locked in with you will fight his way out, kill if he must
You are children but it begins with children
This isn't a trap to earn a piece of respect
Merely a stroke in the masterpiece of haunting

On their way out to the dark, they've cursed you
Cursed the tree and its ornaments
The silence is knifing itself, the silence believes in merciful com-
pared to this
Curses and tears, oh redemption, far flung you are, years in where
you witnessed were not a gleam
It will go beyond tonight, it will go on for a long time, forever for some
Stronger this makes you, no one to prove you're a conqueror
Though it will haunt you

Even the closest voice will want to
You're intruding on self-destruction
You read the walls that have been sealed for years
You need the constant truth of no blood connection
Gain the cough that's unending
Let it release a part of your mind

What makes you, you, beyond weary?
This you face in the room, you do not know yourself
Mornings will come, though there will be hauntings
Let out to a self-proclaimed palace of pain and torment
It has been since you licked the ground
Enjoy the suffering of other prisoners

Had it been that some things are inescapable
As they had early nights of sitting
Threatening heavy voices echoing
Through the leaden wall

III. Ingenuity

Tortoise Blood

How long are we predicting we'll last?
Should we be observed, kept as pets?
By the tortoises that crawl over a century
As our last forty we wept

Are we improving?
Small necessities then enhancing
To find a way to see
Beyond what our lifetimes suppose we should

Is it wrong to like what's like a drop in a bucket?
Trying to turn it away from its speed
Slow to a crawl

Is it wrong to think of ways not to mourn?
To not be painted by death always, to not be defined as so
Only when gone

At last imagining an easier way to live
Or will we be accused of having tortoise blood
Flowing through our veins

I. Calloused Hands

It was with these, in the grit and strain
Hands into earth until the sun sets
These hands that build against the eyes that choose not to look
To make in secret in plain sight
They build layers of thickness, toughening
As the souls of the person, harder skin
Although it could still be wounded when it comes from them
When they are blamed, accused as if they have to choose to do nothing
When it is what they'll leave
Who will see it?

Who will understand?

How could they know what would come of it
None would know
The waves of ignorance and appreciation
Is not why these hands work all their lives
As if they knew nothing more
Yet it takes us away from the dark

These days that allow light in late hours
That bring a way to travel miles in minutes
To reach a person a world away
These calluses on these hands are not shared with the many, in the factory's flat and grey
Instead they are at secrets at a desk

Hunched over, sleep would just be a dream of this so why sleep at all?
These callused hands that create, they share a friend in another,
who should be smooth and unharmed, a sign of mind more than
brawn but toil as well
It is the hand that grabbled the pen to use
From the moment it is young until the arthritis comes
The sitting of the desk eager
Not left until a hand must be patient to pull the person up

What could be written, what's said with these hands, how can it
contend with all the working in life
When it's self was limited to such a short amount
Yet these callused hands, they worked through many nights
More than a word of a child unknowing that has yet to come could say
More perhaps then even a gifted person with far sight could ever know
The hands don't create to expect others gratitude, though to affect
is another matter entirely
No they create to keep us out of the dark into the light
A burning that hardly needs a flame when these hands are given

II. Ruins

For the hands that find it, discover it and perception is widened
For the hands that display it, a symbol of understanding
Is also the hands that move rocks when what's gained again has crumbled
The world throwing it back into the unknown
The hall with no end
Another set of hands long after would find pieces of what's under the rubble
Unsure how many times this was lost to the world, to knowledge and mind
Finding its worth, they would once again shine a light
For these hands are new but their desires old, their desire to display
An earnest symbol that we always seek, our roots are somewhere in the manmade haze
Somewhere among the rubble, where age has become ruins
The new hands see rocks as many hands do
Moving it to find what is lost, as long as they can
To go as all the hands go, searching, even if reaching in a forgotten dark
Continuing to discover that which is lost

III. Museum

Where sadness cannot reach me, its wave overturned
To a world where everything has no meaning from before
It has a value here
The day you wait for otherwise would be snatched away
The mind dreading over it as if it was other worldly hands
Resonate as what's displayed, looking upon you
It dares you to see what others do not, not remnants but what is
existing in front of you
Are these bonds, descriptions of things long past
Are they simply what's left, pressed to the glass, the diagrams of
what had been?

Is it us pressed to the glass
Even more so, stuffed dolls of cotton
Or what we see is as real as us
There's value here
Time well spent
A clearer interpretation of the world we're always guessing
A well with reflections upon its waters
From explorers to conquers
Civilizations that were ours with other names
The individuals that lived in them like me
Animals from all corners of the world seen and unseen
Every step of understanding in this wonder of preserve
Is a greater value of me

The Gardner of Mars

Where there were once oceans
Where the lands once had grass
The gardener, so far from home, scratches his head and sees a
vision
It is here at what first appears barren
Where the shadows hold secrets
Fit for a planet with many lives
Surely his home will hide some in time

But the gardener doesn't want to turn it that way
Nothing to maintain at first glance
Nothing to water and bring life to
Only standing in an empty spa
Wondering now what legacy exist
To a place the color of blood dried

Everything is distant
Everything is gone, the whispers of nothing say
Ones he cannot believe, they are from a small corner of the mind
belonging to madness
One the gardener never lets inside

You can hear it, a planet alive still churning
Enough to turn the concept of death into a romantic dream
Somewhere it is saying for nourishing, that what lives on has chosen
to be hidden
A legacy that had waited to continue

By Candlelight

It was like stepping out of the haze of a dream into the bright lights that flooded
Much different than the candlelight of dim, blind, huddled around pages of words
Too much weight and too much space people complained
Once when such things could still be treasure, once be a worry we could afford
But how far could you truly go without it
For a mind of thoughts is weighed through a lifetime
Heavier is far better than light
For the thought of sight disappear as age comes, is a thought better not to have
But if we deem the monsters we create that make it one without choice
Than better is the time spent, in the candle light dim, acquiring the words and pages
Then to lose sight having never read a word at all

Nailed To A Bulletin

History should be written with a pencil
Equipped with an eraser
Truth hidden in the first writing

If all smart people were smart
We may have peace instead of embezzlement
Less chaos and puppet masters
Innocence maintained

What we know should be said
Words nailed on a bulletin
A little for thought
Just a little hope to recognize

Aware

Why be aware?
It's as much for us as for them
Equal Footing
Why know, why be aware of all things before?
If not to put a gloss over history, if not to make the truth easier to
swallow

It is for this
To know accomplishments and mistakes
To know real truth not just fed truth
To know what it is to live, what it means
Where I stand, where you stand
May have been dirt roads and may now be buildings and may be
nothing once again
 Yet shouldn't we know the ground we stand on?

The good among the bad
Ones who thought your thoughts, lived their days, their years
Cried your years, felt your fears, relieved
Alive during surprising times never thought ready
Like them we live

The Art is Dead?

Sinking into a lonely corner
Are these words no longer needed to describe
To say the form is gone, the art is dead
Is to dam so many souls if not all

How can an insight into our mind
Through the lines of rhyme and their own rhythm
To those with their individual lines
Be considered gone when poetry is life?

Teaching us living, pulling the secrets from our mind
Can you attest to it, can the millions?
Or to the remainder that have never read or listen
How their world will crumble, fall to the ground, like the wings of a
bee needed
Changing our world forever

I. *Against The Forces Of Nature*

Forgive me self that I have never known the name
To beg the question of what is the flicker, what it means when light
is giving out
What it means to be blinked out of existence

These hands toil, thick with unseen blisters, all that is smooth is rough
They are felt crinkling, falling apart, list in thought when I should be
asleep
For every precious moment spent toward some goal, impossible to
be held

Against the test of memory
Against the true silence that the echoes try to reach
Greater movements like chess pieces

Though there is no concern of victor or defeat
Only of the precise movements in chaos
Its natural order

That has not been searched
Yet longest to pose the question of meaning
The greater point, the greater mark

Beyond the eventual, all things unnamed and unfamiliar
Toward a greater thought to question
Facing the forces of nature
Where one does not have to grasp the scene
Only wonder if it's a part of survival, in how we always thought we
would

We've only tried a step in the greater scheme of things, not to
desire there to be no point
Finally it can be called more than a selfish reason

Swirling with one empty that it never gave itself
Built to black if we really look that is what we see
When facing the forces of nature

II. Droplets in The Universe

What are legacies?
The ones we build
The ones we dedicate an entire existence towards
When we've disappeared
Those that carry it watch it crumble, after only several generations
If they carry them at all
Those that go against it and lost wishes for better or for worse
crush anything that survives the blown flicker of the flame of life

What are legacies?
Our need to leave something behind
How long do we expect it there?
Do we fear nothing would be left at all?
Are we droplets in the universe?
Our movements hardly ripples?

Or have we reached a point to find
The definition of what we strived for
To alas have some meaning

A grander thing
Among us the ordered chaos
The violence of creations and ends

To grasp in our hands
Droplets wetting the skin
Seeing how it exists
Wondering what it would be like if it never dried

Have we climbed these thoughts?
If not then can anyone?
For every river or ocean starts with a drop

Perhaps it is the hand that needs to feel it
To wet the skin, even something vast once, thought beyond compre-
hension
To see even it can be changed, even it can build a legacy

One in stone not brittle by tens of thousands of years
As intangible as the forces of nature
A legacy made to last

IV. Transition

There are no clocks in here

Are we looking to leave or we looking to stay
The artificial light has no way of knowing
There are no guide posts here
The doors are shut, if you're lingering in uncertainty
 To you that must seem like a lock
But you're far away from the halls
With the mixture of smells
Perfume, cologne, aftershave, and the breath of exhaustion
What rests in here, perhaps there is a reason for it
More than monotonous, more than the slow churn
I am more
Said to the room without a face
I want to be more
Here, where people's lives and dreams flourish and disintegrate
Where the dim light can be dimmer
The voices are turning into their caves of complaint
You could see it as a place free or imprisoned
The crowds come in and leave but they are never real
So rare is the face and no one waits
The deeds unachieved
Time just a question of place
There are no clocks in here

Conversations of Temporary Solutions

I don't want you to leave, take you anywhere but here
Do not want a tomorrow, let tonight be forever, let tonight be the
end of all things
Let's speak of what is and what's disappearing
In our conversations of temporary solutions
Where the miles driven aren't farther away, the night wished
forever not long enough
But surely from this air we both feel, this temporary freedom, there
is one that is ever lasting
There is one in which we can taste, in which we had waited
Surely it is easy not to turn back, all we have to choose is a way
forward

Two People Seen From A Window or The Last Thoughts Of Love

When he met her it had been in utter fascination
Although their eyes met right away
No white mists in the corners
No dream like fog framing their moment

It had been at a shabby shop
He had already been watching with her back turned
Unbeknownst to her
Short brown hair, large round eyes
Even from the side he was sitting he could tell

She ate with speed as if there was time to make the most of
Yet there was enjoyment there, what he longed for
He hardly remembered the words they spoke to each other
Perhaps because truly he'd already been speaking to her for some
time in his head

Our Awkward World

For once we try to smile with all or heart
Muscles burning
Before an easier laugh came out,
From you across though it wasn't the laugh that you see
Commenting where our open smile was, that we have spinach in
our teeth
We are the awkward ones, if ever we needed a reminder

The ones that call and are told the person is actually busy
We are the ones told we're too old to be fans, too old to cheer
Too young to theorize, to cure
To out of place to be asked for an opinion
No tact to say the right thing at the right time

However there's no one like us
The imitators could never know
They're effort too much
The common thought can be strange
We aren't interested in understanding
Embarrassment would seem our legacy

They're still nothing like us
Awkward isn't our shame
We do not drag it as weight
Chains carried over a lifetime of regret
Our apparent inadequacies is our individuality

We are away from the earth shattering civilization
Though we may be everything they've needed

No brimming shame nipping at our ears, no ripped emptiness in our chest
Realizing this is why it doesn't pain us to smile, there's nothing to
take it away
We've only ever been accepted by the one we would ever need to
We've accepted ourselves

Natural Flavors

The taste is wires like pulling out the stomach
Making me closer to a machine set to rust

While those built from the start are shackled all the same
It's all natural they say

Except we don't know what reality is, so we don't know what we are
Natural, a dismissal of the obsolete

It is supposed to be known not labeled

Instead though an assumption of confusion is that natural law is our
own disbelief in knowledge of ourselves, it's all chaos and sensors,
touches and senses, laying on top of each other. In an orgy of
stillness, rotting of fruition

It's seeped in us so they say. A person dead, philosopher, who'd
written thoughts that could fill a row of bookcases, no one would
ever know it was so had he lived

A world renowned writer, has the answers to nearly everything,
impotent in his intelligence, revered and his own life is broken, into
pieces of jagged jigsaw that he has no way of knowing how to fix
To this there is assurance that it is natural, a sure way to live. That
we should ignore the notions we speak day in day out about. Skin
bags of gases, liquids and chemicals that make up the rest of the
ruthless production of the universe. Mate and reproduce and feel
your head looking toward the ground as the cycle has turned and
you've reached the end

Natural flavors, seep to the top, the first we drink, the first we kiss, the first we miss when they take away essentials we were told we never possessed

Unwritten

Roaches resting on the silverware at night
Whispers in the bedroom
Intruders on the lawn
The children wail for the future unknowingly

Cars move themselves out of park, when no one looks to find a
sparing view
Absence is the meaning of money
As neighborhoods constrict not crumble
Days are numbered warn the news flashes

Trust is a fairy tale we've never believed in
Love is the talk of the town
Futures remain unwritten
Due to all the empty stares that eat the hours

An all the great guidelines of great things
Have been chosen a fate worse than forgotten
To why we question if it's evil
Is still a thing that is chosen?

Leaves a world that is turning
A spate of wonder in which way it's direction?
While the ravaged dog searches for something to eat

The Descent Is Not The End

I have fallen, I have been pushed, I have slipped, stumbled
My thoughts are as clear as they ever were maybe even sharper
but the clouds of what happen seems to allow a fog and I've
allowed it's thickness but no matter where it has dropped me, it
won't be the end
So I will climb
To life
So I will climb
Find a way to perfect on what it is I've set out on every rung, on
every step
So I will climb

To breathe the fresh air that is forbidden here
For you, that waits upon the top, you, that hadn't commented on
where I've found myself below
For you, who has only been waiting for what you thought was
inevitable
My ability to lift myself and join you again

Nexus

The shadows that our forefathers casted upon the fire
Hands that reached to build a world
Instruments that turned what lurked into prey
From the elements they would carve in several directions
Into their own image

It was empires they would build
Looking at the many entities as the reason for their being
Before the storms that time provides
To change all we know, once we claimed we do
It is then that we question, gain and regain
Redefine what it means to be human

To these worlds of cloth and customs, of food and expressions
Taboos upon normalcy lifted
Intricacies developed
Making no place the same and for all our differences
For the hours that chimed uncertainty
For struggles that seemed forever ongoing
We looked upon the stars wondering

If our legacy must be self-contained
Confined to one place or should we dare something greater
More so than the forces of nature or the land that we stand
Are we to continue ever searching?

Even when some history seems to be shrouded in dust
One time has provided with pleasure
If we look at our world, so much we built appeared everlasting

So much now that we've learned as a lesson in time and change
and people

How it pumps something like blood in our veins
This motivation, this inspiration
To be more than the young vigor figure in a greater history
Aged hardly in a blink of an eye, we want to continue to bear what
our forefathers had begun
For that shadow was much longer when it was cast
Made from a flame we must never let flicker out

Towards the nexus we continue
To question ourselves, somewhere closer to further
To not end a journey so early in its walk of morrow

Dreams of Being An Old Man

I would trade the aging couch and the midnight yawn
For the wisdom that should come along
Hand in hand with something bigger than a notch on my belt
A line on the wall
Moving of a season

Rather the waiting of a complex task
A sense of something accomplished
Enwrapped in this world
A true sense of accomplishment

Not withered like the flower
Standing ground, plains of free
Chains of old, broken, buried
Age not torment, balm of relief

The wander is over, sense of home bigger than others
For these dreams can be loved
An expansion it is not, the greater step it can be
The desire is simple though rich in complex

These thoughts of years ahead, these dreams
Are for something bigger in existence
Not the dwindling that comes before the fade away
Just the dreams of a young man aged

www.ingramcontent.com/pod-product-compliance
Lightning Source LLC
LaVergne TN
LVHW051501170726
843492LV00002B/755